THIS BOOK BELONGS

TO:

....

Dinosaurs are
a group of reptiles
that have lived on Earth
for about 245 million
years.

Dinosaur fossils have been found on all seven continents.

The name dinosaur
means
'frighteningly big lizard'

All non-avian
dinosaurs went
extinct about 66
million years ago.

There are roughly 700 known species of extinct dinosaurs.

No one is completely sure how dinosaurs became extinct, but most think that it was because of a massive asteroid (huge rock from space) crashing into the earth, or a gigantic volcanic eruption, or both. It's still a mystery today.

There were survivors
of the extinction :
species of turtle, lizard,
snake, bird and crocodile
can all be traced back
to the Mesozoic era,
they have evolved to
survive on our planet
today.

Many dinosaur
skulls had big holes
that both made
them lighter and
helped to keep
them cool

When dinosaur
bones were first
found hundreds of
years ago by the
Chinese, they
thought they were
the bones of giant
dragons.

The very biggest dinosaurs ate only plants. Those that ate meat were usually much smaller.

A person who studies
dinosaurs is called a
palaeontologist.

The biggest dinosaur
eggs scientists Know of
are the eggs of the
segnosaurus, which were
about 19 inches long

The smallest dinosaur eggs ever found measured about 0.7 inches (smaller than the diameter of a penny)

While most people think that all dinosaurs were very big, the smallest were about the size of chickens, and current estimates place the average dinosaur at about the size of a small car.

The Tyrannosaurus ("Tyrant Lizard") had the longest teeth of any carnivorous dinosaur at 8 inches.

Lizards, turtles,
snakes and crocodiles
all descend from
dinosaurs

Dinosaurs were
the biggest animals
ever to have
walked on earth.

Scientists speculate that some large dinosaurs like the Apatosaurus lived as long as 300 years

Unlike most animals
alive these days,
dinosaurs weren't
warm OR cold blooded.
They were somewhere
in between.

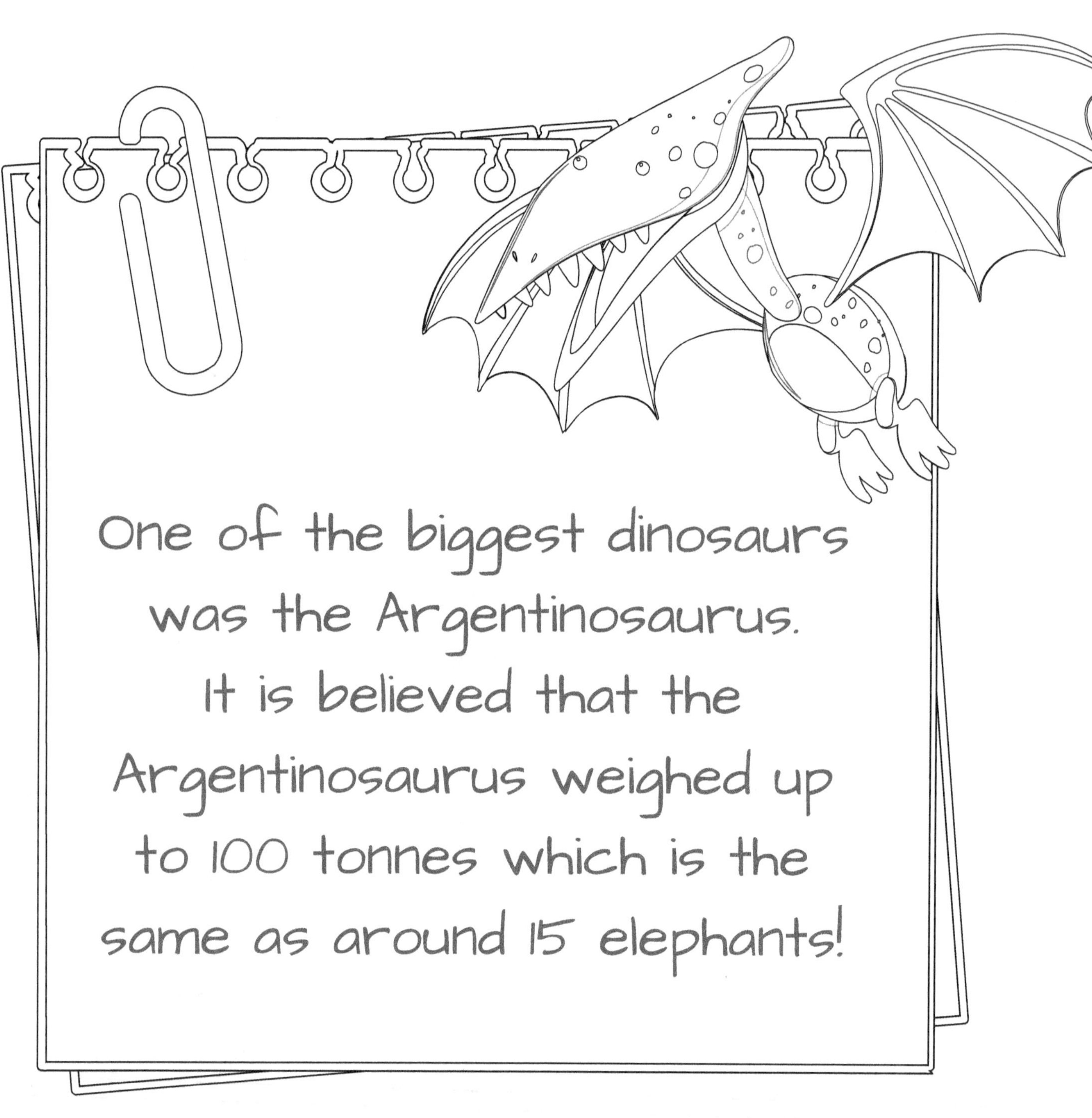

One of the biggest dinosaurs
was the Argentinosaurus.
It is believed that the
Argentinosaurus weighed up
to 100 tonnes which is the
same as around 15 elephants!

Birds descended from a type of dinosaurs known as theropods.

The American explorer Roy Chapman Andrews found the first known dinosaur eggs in Mongolia's Gobi Desert in 1923

Most dinosaurs had
very small brains
and were about as
clever as modern
reptiles

The longest dinosaur name
is
"Micropachycephalosaurus"
This dinosaur would have
lived around 84 - 71 million
years ago.

Many scientists believe that there are still lots of dinosaurs that haven't been discovered yet

Most carnivorous dinosaurs were bipeds, meaning they walked on two feet. Walking on two feet helped them move faster and left their hands free to catch their prey

It has recently
been discovered
that some
dinosaurs even had
feathers.

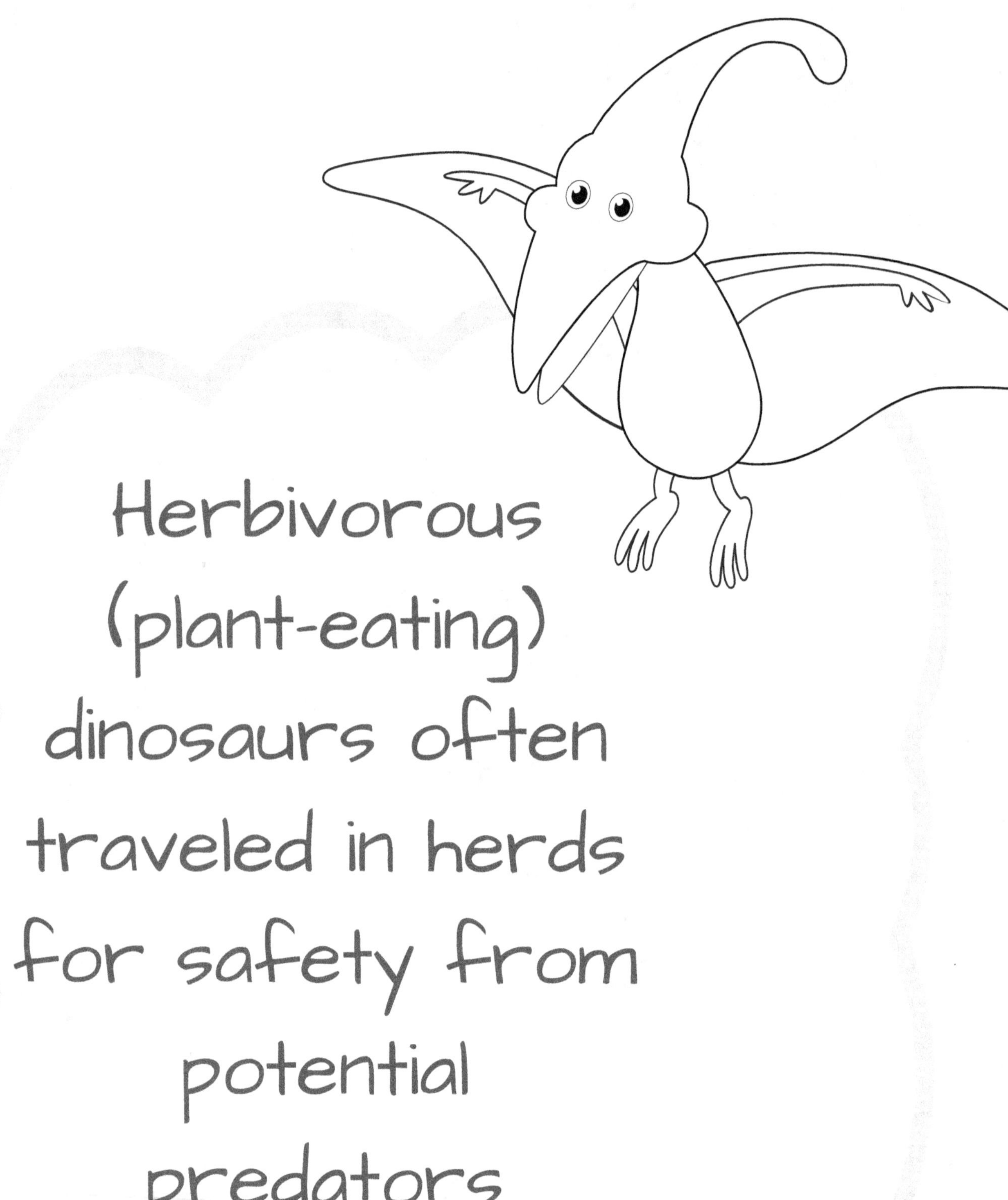

Herbivorous (plant-eating) dinosaurs often traveled in herds for safety from potential predators

One reason that plant-eating dinosaurs grew so big was because they were so greedy. They could eat a huge amount of food very quickly. Sometimes, they swallowed up whole branches without chewing!

Dinosaurs lived on Earth
for a far longer time
than humans have, with
their family trees
stretching back many
millions of years.

My Notes

../.../....